2/92

THREATENED CULTURES

Virginia Luling

Rourke Enterprises, Inc.
Vero Beach, FL 32964

World Issues

Cities in Crisis
Endangered Wildlife
Exploitation of Space
Food or Famine?
Human Rights
International Terrorism
Nuclear Power
Nuclear Weapons
Population Growth

Refugees
Sports and Politics
The Arms Trade
The Energy Crisis
The Environment
The International Debt Crisis
The International Drug Trade
Threatened Cultures
World Health

First published in the
United States in 1990 by
Rourke Enterprises, Inc.
Vero Beach, FL 32964

Text © 1990 Rourke Enterprises, Inc.

Library of Congress Cataloging-in-Publication Data

Luling, Virginia, 1939-
    Threatened cultures/by Virginia Luling.
       p.   cm. — (World issues)
    Includes index.
    Summary: Describes the cultures of certain
indigenous peoples, such as the Bushmen of the
Kalahari and the forest people of Borneo, and examines
how such cultures are threatened and changed by the
encroachment of modern civilization.
    ISBN 0–86592–096–6
    1. Indigenous peoples—Juvenile literature.
2. Culture conflict—Juvenile literature.
[1. Indigenous peoples.   2. Culture conflict.]
I Title.   II. Series: World issues (Vero Beach, Fla.)
GN380.T85 1990   89–34428
306—dc20   CIP
                                                   AC

Printed by Rotolito Lombarda Milan Italy

Cover picture: The Bushmen of the Kalahari are
probably the most badly treated people in the bloody
history of South Africa.
Frontispiece: A Dinka herder watches over his cattle
in the Sudan.

Contents

1 Introduction

What is a culture?

A culture is the way of life of a people. It is what makes them unique, what makes them able to say "we."

Our culture includes how we make our living, what we eat and wear, our laws and customs, our history, our language, our religion, our ideas of what is right and wrong, beautiful and ugly. It is everything we value and believe in, and everything we take for granted and think of as normal.

For me as an individual, my culture has helped to form me as a person, and is an important part of my idea of myself. It is part of my identity. Even if I rebel and reject part or all of it, I will still be marked by it.

There is a sense in which every family has its own culture, made up of shared memories and jokes, ways of celebrating birthdays or other festivities, knowledge of how to do things and where things are kept. The same goes for any group of people – a school, a village, a region. But generally when we talk of a culture, we are referring to a larger group, which we may call a people, a tribe, or a nation.

One of the most important parts of any culture is its language. Through this, people understand each other, and know they belong together and are separate from others who do not understand. Groups who fear they might lose their identity, such as the Welsh in Britain, know how important it is to keep their language.

Human beings have invented an amazing variety of different cultures. Each is an experiment in how to live, a different way of being human. But cultures may be lost, and today more than ever many cultures are in danger of being destroyed. A culture may disappear

Religious figures such as Jokang are an important part of Tibetan culture.

because the people to whom it belongs are all killed or die out (as happened to many tribes in South America). This is plainly a tragedy and, if they are killed off deliberately, a terrible crime – the crime of genocide. But what if the people, or some of them, remain alive but lose their culture? Why should this matter?

From an outsider's point of view the disappearance of any culture detracts from the richness and variety of human life, and deprives the rest of the world of the things they might have learned from it. This is true of a civilization like that of Tibet, with its books, temples and works of art, and also of peoples like the hunters of the tropical forests, who have a tremendously detailed and valuable knowledge of the plants and animals of the forest.

Development or destruction?

To be deprived of one's culture is one of the most painful and destructive experiences for people because it attacks what they value, their pride and their feeling of who they are. This does not mean, of course, that it is bad for people to change or modernize their culture in any way. All cultures change; that is to say, the people to whom they belong adopt new methods and ideas, abandoning old ones. This may be a very slow process, or quite a fast one, but it is inevitable that changes occur. As long as people do not abandon all of their culture at one time, there is continuity as well as change, and they do not lose touch with their past. This is the development of culture. The most important difference between this and the destruction of culture (sometimes called ethnocide) is that in development the peoples themselves are in control and choose what to discard of their culture and what to hold on to, whereas destruction of culture is brought about by outside forces. Keeping your culture does not mean remaining unchanged, but changing in your own way. A threatened culture is one in danger of destruction.

This book will examine some of these threatened cultures: what they are like, and what forces threaten them. Finally it looks at how they can survive.

Who are minorities?

The cultures that are threatened are those of minorities – groups of people who are few in number and have little or no control in their government. This does not include immigrant minorities, such as Hispanics or Asians in the U.S. who belonged to the majority in the country from which they came, though their problems are in some ways similar. The people of threatened cultures are threatened within their own country and have no other country to go to.

The nation-states that make up the modern world nearly all have minority peoples within them. There are many reasons for this; one of the main ones is the great colonization movement in modern times by people of European descent. In other parts of the world, minority peoples have emerged as a result of conquest by a dominant group, either recently or long ago. Thus in China there are fifty-five "national minorities." In Russia, minorities range from European nationalities such as the Ukrainians, to the indigenous hunters and trappers of northern Siberia. Ethiopia has about 100 different peoples in it, most of them conquered at the end of the nineteenth century by the dominant Amhara people. The U.S. has its own native minorities in the many American Indian tribes.

This nomadic family belongs to one of China's fifty-five national minorities.

In other cases, certain groups of people live separated from the rest of the population, either by choice or because they live in remote areas and so have developed distinctive cultures of their own. Examples of this are the "tribal" people of India or the Philippines.

Minorities are also created by the way in which international frontiers are drawn, as in the case of the Kurds of the Middle East, who are split among Iran, Iraq and Turkey and rejected by all three countries. The nation-states of modern Africa, for instance, had their frontiers set up by the colonial powers of Europe, without much regard for the people who were actually living there. (You only need to look at a map of Africa to see that they were drawn with a ruler; people on the ground do not divide up in this way.) Hence African states are groups of peoples, large and small, trying to live under one government, and many African peoples are divided between two or more states. This can lead to devastating conflicts.

Finally there are those peoples who are minorities wherever they live, like the Jews through most of history, or the Gypsies.

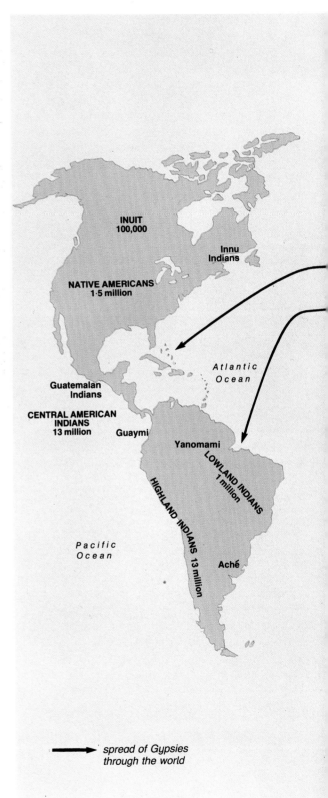

INUIT
100,000

Innu
Indians

NATIVE AMERICANS
1·5 million

Atlantic
Ocean

Guatemalan
Indians

CENTRAL AMERICAN
INDIANS
13 million   Guaymi

Yanomami

LOWLAND INDIANS 1 million

HIGHLAND INDIANS 13 million

Pacific
Ocean

Aché

→ spread of Gypsies
through the world

Above *Changing boundaries has devastating consequences: the Kurds are split among three countries and many are now refugees.*

Right *Some of the world's threatened cultures.*

Main Groups of Threatened Cultures (1988)

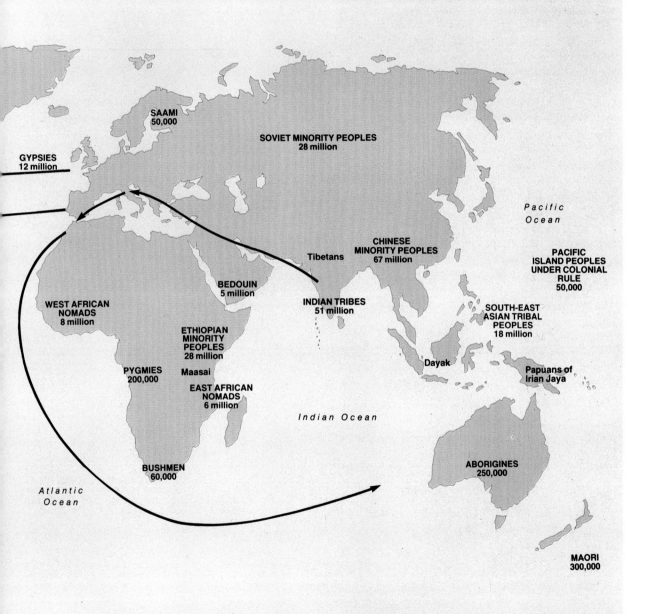

SAAMI
50,000

SOVIET MINORITY PEOPLES
28 million

GYPSIES
12 million

Pacific
Ocean

CHINESE
MINORITY PEOPLES
67 million

Tibetans

PACIFIC
ISLAND PEOPLES
UNDER COLONIAL
RULE
50,000

BEDOUIN
5 million

INDIAN TRIBES
51 million

SOUTH-EAST
ASIAN TRIBAL
PEOPLES
18 million

WEST AFRICAN
NOMADS
8 million

ETHIOPIAN
MINORITY
PEOPLES
28 million

PYGMIES
200,000   Maasai

Dayak

Papuans of
Irian Jaya

EAST AFRICAN
NOMADS
6 million

Indian Ocean

ABORIGINES
250,000

Atlantic
Ocean

BUSHMEN
60,000

MAORI
300,000

Source: Survival International

9

2 The indigenous peoples

Until the last 500 years of the two million or so years that human beings have inhabited the planet Earth, Europeans, or "white people," were mainly confined to the comparatively small part of it that we call Europe. But in the fifteenth century, voyagers from Europe set out to "discover" other regions, and it was often not long before discovery led to attempted conquest. While rich countries such as China had the power to negotiate and deal with Europeans as traders, smaller or weaker states gave way. Peoples who lived in scattered family or tribal groups had no chance at all against the newcomers with their guns and armies.

Europeans rarely doubted their right to rule over these "new" lands; the inhabitants, with their strange ways, seemed to them to be clearly inferior, needing to be ruled and civilized, or only fit to be servants and laborers. The names they used to refer to them were nearly always scornful. Even the word *native* – meaning simply a person who is born in a country – has come to have a contemptuous ring. During the following centuries, the population of Europe spilled over into these newly conquered countries. The result for the peoples who lived in them was frequently disastrous. When they were not murdered, they often died from diseases to which they had no immunity, such as flu or measles, which they caught from the Europeans. Some settlers were happy to kill off the natives. Gentler souls simply assumed that they were doomed to die out anyway, that this was on the whole a good thing, but that one should help them to do so as painlessly as possible.

So today large parts of the earth are dominated by inhabitants of European descent, while the people to whom those lands originally belonged live on scraps of their former territory, or as second-class citizens among the majority. When these countries gained independence from colonizers such as Britain, Spain and Portugal, it was the descendants of the colonists who became independent, not those of the original inhabitants.

The Portuguese slaughtered the Botocoudo Indians when they colonized Brazil.

Native Americans

The American lands contained many flourishing societies when Columbus and his men landed here in 1492, mistakenly thinking that they were in the East Indies (which is why we call Native Americans "Indians"). In the highlands of the Andes and in Central America, complex states and empires with stone-built cities and temples had existed for many years – the Maya, the Aztec, the Inca. To the north and south smaller groups of people, tribes of a few hundred or thousand, or family bands, lived by hunting, farming and fishing in ways suited to the various climates and environments of the two continents.

Many people's image of North American Indians is based on what they see in Westerns. But much of what has been shown (Big Chiefs, tomahawks, happy hunting grounds and so on) is either out of date or never had much to do with reality. People think of the Indians as belonging to the past, but they are very much in existence today. Yet their cultures and attitudes to life are still profoundly different in many ways from those of non-native Americans, and to this day efforts to make them the same –

The Caribbean Indians, shown here offering gifts to Christopher Columbus in 1492, were wiped out within a century of his landing.

to assimilate them – have failed. This is especially true of their attitude to land. Indian cultures value collaboration and sharing, rather than each person getting rich separately. They see the land as their mother, or as something given by their creator, not something that can be divided into lots to be bought and sold.

The conquerors of North America, who built up the great nations of Canada and the United States, defeated the Indian tribes one by one. Treaties were made with them, safeguarding their rights to their lands, but again and again the treaties were broken. Now the tribes of the U.S., like most of the Canadian ones, have been left with small areas of land as reservations. This land is nearly always the most barren and useless, the land that the settlers did not want. Reservation Indians are the poorest people in the United States. Less than a tenth of Indian land has any reserves of gas or minerals. And when such reserves are present, it does not necessarily make the people rich. The result can be quite the opposite.

11

> We believe the Creator placed us on our land to remain on and care for it. Our sacred prayer and offering sites cannot be abandoned or replaced. This religious teaching is our ultimate purpose in life.
>
> *Betty Tso, Navaho Indian*

For instance, 2,000 Navaho Indians are today holding out against a government attempt to move them from their lands in the area known as Big Mountain, to make a large area of the reservation available for the mining of coal and uranium. Since 1974 all repairs to homes or farm buildings have been forbidden in the area. Hundreds of Navaho families have been moved to nearby towns, but the majority have already lost their new homes and, unable to return to the reservation, are living in great poverty. Still the protestors hold on.

Today there is a strong determination among these Native Americans – as they are now properly known – to stand up for their rights and their identity, whether they still follow their old traditions very closely like the Navaho of Big Mountain, or have a more "modern" way of life.

Many Native Americans are demanding their rights to land and their culture; here a Navaho argues his people's case to the press.

The Indians of Guatemala: victims of a struggle

The descendants of the people who made the great states of Central America and the Andean highlands have, since they were first conquered by the Spaniards, been deprived of nearly all their land, and forced back into the most barren and remote areas. Today most of them are very poor peasants. Yet they have clung stubbornly to their cultures, though despised by both the rulers and middle classes (who are mainly of Spanish or other European descent).

Often Indians are caught up in the murderous struggle going on in present-day states between right-wing governments and left-wing

These Guatemalan Indians were among the terrified thousands who fled the bloodshed and political struggle of their country and now live as refugees in Mexico.

and Communist rebels. Nowhere is that struggle more horrific than in Guatemala. During the 1970s and 1980s the army and "death squads," who wear no uniform, have been killing not only Communists but anyone belonging to a group that might conceivably be suspected of sympathizing with the rebels. Among their victims are students, priests, and Indians.

The Indians of Guatemala make up over half the country's population of eight and a half million. They are the descendants of the Mayas, the builders of the great cities now hidden in the Central American jungles. They have lost nearly all the land they once held and now either farm tiny plots of barren soil or work as laborers for starvation wages in the coffee, banana or sugar plantations of rich landowners or foreign companies.

This report is based on the testimony in 1982 of an Indian woman, who had fled the bloodshed of Guatemala for safety in Mexico:

> She and other villagers were carrying bags down the road when they met the soldiers. The soldiers demanded chickens and other things, and asked them about the guerrillas. Frightened by this, she and others threw down their bags and ran. She, her husband and children hid, then watched as the soldiers started to kill people. In all, twenty-five people were killed as they fled down the road. Children's throats were cut, and women were hit with machetes. Old people also were killed. She and her family walked to Mexico in two days, during which time they almost died from hunger.

Today a journalist writes:

> The mountain trails . . . are littered with the debris of a culture – earthenware cooking pots smashed, weaving equipment broken, machetes bent double and Indian clothing ripped to shreds. Skulls and human bones litter the sites of massacres. In many communities every house has been burned to the ground.

Some Indians do indeed join the rebel guerillas, hoping this is the way to freedom. But the guerrillas too have killed Indians who failed to support them.

There seems little hope for the Indians of Guatemala today, unless their government changes completely. However, in other Central and South American countries, Indian groups have been able to organize, though against heavy odds. In Panama, for instance, the Guaymi people organized a protest against a

The Guaymi Indians of Panama protested successfully against plans for a copper mine that would have robbed them of their land.

huge copper mine which, if it had been opened, would have destroyed much of what is left of their land. In their negotiations with the government, the Guaymi Indians managed to raise support from many people both in

Guatemalan Indians now fear to wear the splendid costume that identifies them.

Panama and abroad. The plans for the copper mine were eventually canceled.

At the white man's school
What are the children taught?
Are they told of the battles our people
   fought?
Are they told how our people died?
Are they told why our people cried?
Australia's true history is never read,
But the black man keeps it in his head.

Aborigine poem

Aborigines had to remind Australia of its black history at the 200 years' celebrations.

Australia's Aborigines: "nothing to celebrate"

In 1988 the Australian nation celebrated its 200th birthday, the anniversary of the first British settlement in 1788. But there was one group of people in Australia who declared that they had "nothing to celebrate in 88." These were the Aborigines, as their conquerors called them, meaning "those who were there from the beginning."

The past of the Australian Aborigines, according to recent research, may go back as far as 100,000 years. At the time of the English

colonization there were at least 750,000 Aborigines, speaking hundreds of different languages. They lived by hunting, fishing and collecting wild plants, having an intimate knowledge of the land and many ingenious ways of using what it provided. But the land to them was not only their source of livelihood, it was something sacred, an immense book on which was written the story of their people from the beginning, the Dreamtime, when the divine ancestors, who were both human and animal in nature, shaped the land and everything in it. And yet these people, whose attachment to their land was so strong, were considered by

The shapes in this Aboriginal wall painting symbolize the ancestral legends and the Aboriginal people's struggle for land.

the colonists to have no right to the land at all, because instead of farming fixed plots they were nomads, moving from place to place. No treaties with the Aborigines were broken, for none were ever made. Over the next 150 years, in spite of their desperate resistance, the Aborigines were pushed off the land. Thousands died – massacred by settlers, or from diseases caught from the whites. Others were removed to reserves.

17

At the beginning of the twentieth century, people believed that the Aborigines were disappearing; they were "a dying race." By the 1930s their numbers were down to 70,000. However, in the last forty years their population has risen and they now number at least 200,000. In the north and west of Australia most keep their social and religious traditions, though they no longer live entirely by hunting and gathering. Those in the south and east (generally of mixed descent) live mainly in the cities and towns; having lost their old languages and cultures, they are attempting to build up a new sense of identity as Aborigines.

However, Aborigines remain the poorest group in Australia today. City slums, fringe camps near country towns, and remote reserves house uprooted populations, living on welfare or in hope of casual work. Aborigines are also probably the most frequently imprisoned people in the world. A particular scandal has been the number of deaths of Aboriginal people – mainly young men – while in police custody. The number of known cases between 1980 and the end of 1988 was 108: according to the police these were suicides, but many of their families suspect they died by violence.

Today there is a growing movement among the Aborigines to regain their identity and pride. One of their most important demands is for land rights – the right to control some part of the territory that was once taken from them, especially the sacred sites of the Dreamtime ancestors. This brings them into conflict with (among others) the mining companies, including Rio Tinto Zinc, the same company that intended to mine copper on the land of the Guaymi in Panama.

A sign of hope lies in the many organizations set up by Aboriginal people themselves, such as community schools, where Aboriginal children are taught their own traditions and languages as well as a curriculum in English.

During their protests at the 1988 celebrations, the Aboriginal people's slogan was "We have survived."

Today Aborigines remain the poorest group of people in Australia. Many live dejectedly in fringe camps outside towns.

3 Modern colonizers

Colonizing of one people by another did not begin with the expansion of Europe and it has not ended with the fading of the European empires. In this chapter we look at two examples of how it still goes on.

Mystery and Marxism

The land of Tibet, in high mountains between India and China, has long seemed mysterious to the rest of the world. The old Chinese Emperors claimed overlordship of Tibet, though most of them made no attempt to enforce it. Through most of its history Tibet was independent from China, and the Tibetan people are, in fact, quite different from the Chinese in culture, language, religion and in looks.

In 1949 the Chinese army entered Tibet; however, it was not the old China of the Emperors that took over, but the new People's Republic. The Chinese wanted to control Tibet in order to strengthen their frontier with India, because of the valuable minerals that can be mined there, and because it is a large, comparatively empty country that could be used to take their own spare population. (It has also been used for testing nuclear weapons.) What followed was not only the conquest of a country but the clash of two totally different sets of ideas about the world and what life is about: the Buddhist religion, which forms the core of Tibetan culture, and the Marxist Communism of the new China.

These farmers' children in Tibet are heirs to an ancient culture, now under threat from China.

Buddhism teaches that the world we know is only a temporary appearance, a kind of lightshow, and that salvation lies in passing through this to the timeless "oneness" that lies behind it by following the way of the Buddha and other great teachers. But for the Communist government that now came to rule over Tibet, the only reality was the present and what mattered was material progress. Religion was regarded as a superstition that must be abolished.

In Tibet there were land-owning nobles, and peasant farmers and herders; but the greatest power belonged to the great monasteries. The people most revered were the chief monks, the *Lamas*, who were mystics and teachers of the Buddha's way. The chief of these, and so the ruler of Tibet, was the Dalai Lama. The monasteries were centers for the study of meditation and philosophy, as well as painting, sculpture, embroidery, dance, chant and ritual. They possessed most of the wealth and power

Pilgrims arrive to pray at one of Tibet's many Buddhist temples.

while the ordinary people, the peasants and herders, had to work for the monks and the nobles and pay taxes to them. On the other hand, any man could become a monk, and any woman a nun. Most families tried to get at least one son into a monastery. In this way the sons of poor peasants could become great and powerful.

The Chinese believed they were liberating the Tibetans from their "backwardness" and from the tyranny of the monks and all that they represented. But they were not content to make the monasteries less powerful and wealthy, they were determined to abolish them altogether. Of the 6,000 or so monasteries,

Anger at Chinese rule reached fever pitch in 1988 when robed Tibetan monks led riots in protest at the suppression of their Buddhist religion.

all but a dozen were destroyed; the monks and nuns were forced to renounce their vows, and were often imprisoned or killed.

There was an attempt at rebellion by the Tibetans and, in the war that followed, over a million Tibetans were killed. The Dalai Lama fled across the frontier into India, and many Tibetans followed him.

In Tibet, as all over China during the cultural revolution of the 1960s, there were particularly

21

violent attacks on old ways and all who clung to them. It was at this time that most of the works of art and manuscripts of Tibet were destroyed, or taken out of the country to be sold to foreign dealers. One man described how the people of his village were ordered to pull down their local monastery and shrine; the Buddhist scriptures that had been kept in the shrine were mixed with manure and spread on the fields:

> Many people were crying and fainting while they did this, and as a result the caretaker of the monastery went out of his mind.

Today, although for a while government control did seem to be relaxing, anyone suspected of opposition to Chinese rule still faces prison and torture. The main temples have been rebuilt, and a few monks once again carry out the rituals and study the ancient philosophy, but only in their spare time. During the daylight hours their job is to show the tourists around. Some Tibetans feel that the Chinese tolerance of religion is really only a show for the tourists.

The greatest threat to Tibetan culture today, however, is the number of Chinese people who are encouraged by their government to settle in Tibet. If this process continues, the Tibetans will become a minority in their own country.

Even a generation after the Chinese moved in, Tibetans remain loyal to their religion and to the Dalai Lama. This was shown when, in 1987 and again in 1988, in Tibet's capital, Lhasa, there were demonstrations and riots by Tibetans led by young monks. Meanwhile the Dalai Lama remains in exile, continuing to plead, not that Tibet should become a country wholly independent from China, but simply that Tibetans be allowed to practice freely their religion and way of life.

West Papua and Indonesia

When the Dutch empire in the East Indies came to an end after the Second World War, Indonesia, a collection of islands dominated by the largest and most heavily populated ones, Java and Sumatra, became an independent state. Soon, under a military government, Indonesia began to do its own colonizing.

The great island of New Guinea had been divided during the colonial period between the Dutch and British empires. The British half passed to Australia, and is now independent as Papua New Guinea. The Dutch half, West Papua or West Irian, with its wide untouched forests and rich mines of copper, gold and other minerals, was taken over by Indonesia with the support of the United Nations and renamed Irian Jaya.

The people of New Guinea, known as the Papuans, are utterly different in both culture and appearance from the dominant Javanese. Like the other tribal peoples of the Indonesian islands, they are considered by Indonesian government doctrine to be "backward, alien and isolated"; they are to be educated and "Indonesianized." According to one government document, in order to bring them "up to a par with the rest of the country," children "will be separated from their parents to keep them from settling into their parents' lifestyle."

The program of transmigration, moving huge numbers of settlers from overcrowded Java and the inner islands to the less populated areas, threatens to overwhelm the Papuan people and make them a minority in what was their own land. The forests of West Papua are being cut down for their valuable timber. The Asmat tribe of the southern forests are world famous for their intricate wood carvings, but today many of them have been forcibly moved to the coast, where they are made to labor for logging companies, often paid only with tobacco and cheap clothing.

When the Papuan peoples have tried to resist the government takeover, their rebellion has been quelled by attacks on and bombing of their villages. Tens of thousands of Papuan villagers have been killed; 12,000 to 13,000 thousand refugees are now living in camps over the border in Papua New Guinea. And the war continues.

This man is one of the Moni people of Irian Jaya. Like the other tribal peoples of Indonesia, they are despised by the Indonesians who, under a military government, colonized their territory.

4 Herders and travelers

No cultures are more threatened in the modern world than those of the pastoral nomads: people who live by herding animals, living largely on their milk and meat, and who travel over long distances in order to find grazing land and water for them.

The nomadic way of life is particularly well suited to land like the Sahel – a belt of semi-desert in northern Africa – which is too dry for farming, and where grass and other plants flourish only when rain falls.

Yet this way of life is under heavy attack. Governments tend to consider it old-fashioned, "primitive" and "irrational," though nomads always have good reason for their movements. An official in northern Kenya was reported recently as saying that his government "would no longer tolerate nomadism."

The chief problem of pastoral nomads is that

The Khazak of China and the USSR are one of central Asia's nomadic tribes.

generally the laws of the states they live in do not recognize that they have any right over the land they use. Often it is considered the property of the state. Thus it can be used or given away without consulting the nomads themselves. Turning other parts of their range into nature reserves means that they cannot use that land for grazing. Sometimes projects for drilling wells that are intended to benefit the herders lead to trouble instead. Too many

Many Tuareg of northwest Africa try to maintain their traditional herding life.

people and animals crowd around the new wells – which are not governed by the tribal laws that control access to older wells – so the land there becomes overgrazed and barren. On top of all this, severe droughts during the 1970s and 1980s have brought many African herding peoples near to ruin.

25

The Maasai

Perhaps the most famous of the African pastoral peoples are the Maasai, ". . . the warriors, the aristocrats, the lion-killers, the herdsmen, the drinkers of blood and milk and the carriers of tall spears." When the explorer Joseph Thomson, who wrote these words, traveled through their country in 1883, the Maasai were the undisputed lords of the East African plains. Striding with their spears and leather cloaks behind their magnificent herds of cattle, they could afford to despise the tribes of farmers living around about them, who had to grub in the dirt for their living. Today they still keep obstinately to their traditions. To the tourists who visit East Africa they are a major attraction, but to the governments of Kenya and Tanzania, under which they live, they are an obstacle to "progress."

Cattle are the most important thing in the world to the Maasai; they are killed for meat only on special occasions. Milk is their everyday food, and they also eat grain and other foods that they grow or buy.

The traditional political system of the Maasai was highly democratic; there were no kings or chiefs, but all the elders in a locality met together to judge disputes and discuss policies. Land was the common property of the people in each Maasai tribe.

During the colonial period, the Maasai country was divided between Kenya and what was then Tanganyika. It was during this time that the Maasai first saw large parts of their land taken from them. Otherwise, they were mainly left to go their own way; very few of

Young Maasai warriors in Kenya dance to please tourists.

Above *Maasai prize their cattle above all else, but pasture is getting scarce.*

Below *Unable to live by herding alone, many Maasai now look for work in towns.*

them ever went to school or got a modern education. Consequently , when the two nations became independent in the 1960s (and Tanganyika became Tanzania), few of them were able to become part of the new national governments. So they still found themselves being ruled by others – this time by the sons of the farmers they used to look down on.

More and more Maasai land has been taken over for private farms and ranches, for government projects or for wildlife parks. Often this is the richest, well-watered land where they used to take their herds in the dry season, so they are forced to use the poorer land all year round, and the grass becomes used up. A few Maasai have themselves become wealthy ranchers in the modern way, but this only leaves even less land for the rest. Others have had to give up their herds altogether and go to the towns to get what work they can.

Arctic herders

A very different kind of herding is still carried on near the Arctic Circle. Reindeer are herded for meat, and in some regions for milk, by several of the northern minority peoples of the USSR, and by one people living mainly in western Europe – the Saami. This is their name for themselves, and it is now generally used, though by outsiders they were formerly known as the Lapps.

The Saami have lived in the northern part of Scandinavia for at least a thousand years. In the beginning, they were hunters of wild reindeer. Their herding is not especially primitive; in fact it is a comparatively modern development, dating from the sixteenth and seventeenth centuries, when the herds of wild reindeer started to diminish and the people could no longer live by hunting alone. Not all the Saami are reindeer herders – the majority in fact are farmers or fisherfolk – but a good many still drive the herds from winter to summer pastures and back each year.

Despite the fact that society has done its best to make folk aware of national boundaries, I feel really at home when I'm sitting with the Valkeapää family on the shores of Great Luulaja Lake in Sweden, discussing the harmful effects of the power plant being built there. Ought I to bear in mind that we belong to different nationalities, when I sit with my nieces and nephews in Guovdageaidnu in Norway?

Nils-Aslak Valkeapää
Saami singer from Finland

Saami country was colonized from the south by Russians and Scandinavians over the centuries, and today it is divided among Norway, Sweden, Finland and the USSR. Each of these countries has its own set of laws regulating Saami herding and has imposed its own

The land of Saami herders in the Arctic is under threat from many directions.

language and culture. But the borders that have been imposed upon them mean little to the Saami. The Saami today still live on a good deal of their traditional land and have the right to form their own organizations. Yet as a culture and a people they face many pressures. Their land is threatened by industrial developments, the rivers by hydroelectric dams, and the forests by the logging industry. These encroachments, together with laws limiting the sizes of herds and the number of people who may live off them, drive many Saami away from the herding life. There are now more Saami in the towns of southern Sweden or Norway than there are in the Saami lands in these countries. In the towns they are in danger of losing touch with their culture and people.

The latest disaster to hit the Saami was the fallout from the explosion of the Chernobyl nuclear plant in Russia in 1986. Blown by the winds, the fallout contaminated the moss on which the reindeer graze, so their meat could not be eaten, and huge numbers of the herds had to be slaughtered and buried. The herders received government compensation, but it is pointless for them to rear their animals merely to have them destroyed. However, the Saami have shown in the past that they can adapt their culture to changing circumstances in order to survive and will continue to do so.

The travelers

Herders move camp because they must follow their animals, but in many parts of the world there are nomads of another kind, who move in order to buy and sell. The ones we know best in the Western world are the people we call Gypsies, or travelers. To themselves they are travelers, Rom, Romanichals, Sinte, Cale, Manouche, and other names. They are looked upon by the rest of the world in two opposing ways: as romantically mysterious and exciting, or as dirty undesirables with criminal tendencies. Perhaps this is because they represent for us a kind of freedom that people both long for and resent.

The Gypsies first came to Europe from India by way of the Middle East, arriving in the sixteenth century. They are now to be found

A Gypsy woman, an outcast of European society, tells fortunes in the street.

in every European country, as well as in the Americas, both north and south, and Australia. Through the centuries they have lived by making and selling things that people needed (such as pots and pans), by trading (especially in horses) and as entertainers. As fortune tellers they can cash in on their reputation for being different and mysterious.

Some have been settled house-dwellers for generations (there are Gypsy quarters in some European towns), but most have always led a traveling life. They are particularly famous as musicians, able to adopt the styles of different countries and make them their own. The Flamenco music and dancing, for instance, that many people think of as typical of Spain, is in fact Gypsy music. One of the most famous jazz musicians of recent times, Django Reinhardt, was a French Gypsy.

Living among the peoples of Europe but never belonging to them, obstinately keeping to their own ways and determined to be their own masters, the Gypsies have always met with intense prejudice, and at times have suffered the most terrible persecution. In England and elsewhere during the seventeenth century, laws were passed condemning all Gypsies to death. The last great persecution was in Hitler's Germany, where Gypsies (like Jews) were held to be sub-human, a "disease." Somewhere between 250,000 and 500,000 of them were killed in concentration camps.

The threats to their way of life today are less violent, but still continue. Many of the old trades by which they used to live are no longer wanted. One of the occupations they have taken up instead is collecting and recycling scrap metal (an essential job for industry and the community). Often, however, Gypsies are reduced to taking social security money, a thing they particularly hate, because it takes away their cherished independence.

The chief threat to their way of life in western Europe today is not being allowed anywhere to camp. In order to carry on their trades, they need to be able to stay in one place for a reasonable length of time. In the past, even if they were distrusted, there was little interference if they stayed on a road verge or a common for several weeks. Now there are regulations everywhere forbidding them to camp, and they are constantly harassed and moved on. Where special campsites have been set up for them (often on choice sites such as next to the municipal dump or under a highway), they are too few, so the campers dare not move in case they cannot find another stopping place. So the Gypsies become divided into those who no longer move at all, and those who are never able to stop.

Gypsies today have formed a number of organizations to demand enough camping places and other rights, so that they can continue to live as an independent people.

Gypsies today use modern trailers but are often forced to live in dirty and unpleasant surroundings.

5
The last of the hunters

> You people go to all that trouble working and planting seeds but we don't have to do that. All these things are there for us; the ancestors left them for us.
>
> *Aboriginal woman*

Nomadic people of another kind are those who live by hunting and collecting wild plants; these are known as hunter-gatherers. This was once the way of life of the whole human race, but there are few peoples left today who practice it. The Australian Aborigines all led this sort of life at the time the British settlers arrived, but few of them hunt or gather plants now, and no Aborigines depend entirely on it.

Outsiders generally think that such a way of life, burdened by few possessions (since everything must be carried) and constantly hunting for food, must be poor and miserable. In fact, hunter-gatherers are generally well fed, and spend far fewer hours a day in getting their food than a farmer does.

But one of the things that makes the hunting and gathering way of life difficult in the over-crowded modern world is that a very large stretch of country is required to support even a few people. Hence more and more of these peoples have been crowded out of their hunting grounds, and have to find other ways of surviving. If they are fortunate, they find ways that allow them to keep their independence; but too often they are reduced to becoming cheap laborers for others, or dependent on hand-outs. The remaining hunters have hung on in places that are either too barren or too cold to farm, or deep in the wild forests. Today even those places are being taken over by the modern world.

One of the last peoples to live mainly by hunting and gathering, the pygmy people of Central Africa will have to change their way of life if the forests are destroyed.

The Bushmen of the Kalahari

Before the white people came, we did what our hearts wanted. We lived in different places, far apart, and when our hearts wanted to travel, we traveled. We were not poor. We had everything we could carry. No one told us what to do. Now white people tell us to stay in this place. There are too many people. There's no food to gather. Game is far away and people are dying of tuberculosis; but when I was a little girl, we left sickness behind us when we moved.

I loved to follow my mother. The two of us would be right beside each other ... My mother would open the baobab fruit and ask if we wanted some. Even if you hadn't worked, if hunger grabbed you, you could eat. And when we used up all the food and the year turned hard and hot, we traveled to another place. Those

things we did, long ago, before we knew about money. Now we live at Tsumkwe. Here we eat one thing – mealie meal; and mealie meal and I hate each other.

These are the words of !Nai, a woman belonging to the Bushmen people in Namibia. The Bushmen are a cluster of peoples scattered in the Kalahari desert of southern Africa, which spans southeastern Angola, northeastern Namibia, Botswana, and the northern Cape Province of the Republic of South Africa, an area about seven times the size of Great Britain.

The Bushmen were the original inhabitants of the southern part of Africa, but since other peoples moved in, the Bushmen have probably been the group most badly treated in all the bloody history of South Africa, with its wars between black and white. Everybody hunted, killed and enslaved them. Most Bushmen in the southern African countries today work for starvation wages on farms, or wander in desperate search for work.

Left *Forced from their land, many Bushmen today are dependent on hand-outs or work for starvation wages.*

Below *The Bushmen hunters have lost nearly all their hunting grounds.*

The Ju/Wasi of Western Namibia were among the last of the Bushmen to keep their hunter-gatherer way of life. Up to the 1950s they lived in small groups, the men skillfully hunting animals, the women, like !Nai and her mother, collecting plant foods.

By the 1970s, however, much of what had been their country had been assigned to other people, and they had gathered around the government outpost at Tsumkwe, where some found work but most lived on hand-outs of "mealie meal" (maize meal) and sugar. Many of the young men have found a way out of this dead end by being recruited into the army of South Africa, which rules Namibia, to fight against the SWAPO (South West Africa People's Organization) rebels; this could prove a bad choice in the long run, if the rebels succeed in gaining power.

While they were at Tsumkwe, some of the people, including !Nai, were hired to take part in a film, *The Gods Must Be Crazy*. This told the story of a band of Bushmen living a free life in the wilderness, and who rejected "crazy" modern civilization. The film was a tremendous success in the cities of the world. But in reality there are no Bushmen living like that now; certainly the people at Tsumkwe do not.

Now 500 or so of the Ju/Wasi, with help from an aid organization, are taking up farming and

Young Bushmen escape the poverty at Tsumkwe by becoming soldiers in the South African army.

herding a few cattle and goats, in an effort to be independent and gain their own living. But this is threatened by a plan to use the area as a wildlife reserve for tourists and wealthy big-game hunters, with some "authentic" Bushmen hunter-gatherers as an added attraction. In reality, the Bushmen no longer have enough land to maintain all of them by hunting and gathering, nor does the generation of Bushmen who have grown up at government settlements still have the old skills.

The Aché – the hunters hunted

One of the last of the hunting and gathering peoples in South America is the Aché people of the forests of eastern Paraguay. They are known for their extraordinary skill with bow and arrow, and for their poetry and song. But in recent times their forest has been invaded by loggers, ranchers and settlers, many of whom thought of the Aché as no better than vermin to be wiped out. Like the Bushmen and

Those Aché Indians who have escaped being slaughtered live in sickness and despair.

the Aborigines before them, the Aché hunters were themselves hunted down, their children were taken by the invaders and used as slaves.

A report of one raid by employees of cattle ranchers reads:

This raid was organized towards the end of August 1971 . . . some specialists in killing Achés were contracted for the purpose . . . It was carried out with machete knives, as proudly described by the killers themselves. There were between 12 and 20 killed, some of them most probably the mothers of captured children. At least five small children were captured alive.

The reservations into which some captured Aché were herded were described as being "concentration camps," where they lived in sickness and despair.

35

Today there are no more Aché in the forest. About 400 of them live in four small settlements, where they now have some freedom. They are growing crops, and trying to keep their rights to at least part of the forest so that they can go on hunting there. However, a large-scale development and settlement project threatens to take that away from them too. As many as 100 Aché are said to be working for Paraguayan families, practically as slaves.

Hunters of the far north

The Innu Indians of Labrador, Canada, one of the few remaining hunting and fishing peoples in North America, are not suffering like the Aché, but they too are experiencing an invasion. Their way of life has been disrupted since the Canadian government allowed the Dutch, West German and British air forces to use an air base at Goose Bay in their territory for low-flying exercises. The noise of the planes frightens off the animals, making hunting impossible. Now the Canadian government is threatening to construct a huge NATO training base at Goose Bay, which will – if it goes forward – destroy altogether the Innu way of life, and with it the people's independence.

In September and October 1988, about 200 Innu broke into the air base and set up a protest camp there; one family camped on a bombing range. They made this statement:

> ... present attempts to add a full NATO military base to the present low-level flying and practice bombing activities is but another in a continuing series of illegal activities on our land. The activities are illegal because this is Innu land. We have never signed a treaty or other agreement giving Canada rights on our land. Elders in our camp hunted on the very runway now occupied by warplanes from European countries.

In the struggle for their land, the Innu have become allied with another Indian people, the Dene, and with the Canadian Inuit (who are also known as Eskimo, a name they very much dislike). Together they are campaigning for self-government. They hope that one day they, and only they, will decide whether they want the coal mines, oil companies and military bases that have invaded the Arctic, and which have brought disruption and pollution as well as jobs and money.

But many of these people now live not only by hunting but also by trapping animals for the sale of their furs. This trade was introduced by the white people for the European market, and now many Indians and Inuit depend on it. Today many people condemn the trapping of animals for fur as cruel; if it is banned, the Indians and Inuit may lose this source of livelihood, and it will be hard to find another.

> Our land is everything to us. It is the only place where we remember the same things together.
>
> *Cheyenne Indian*

The hunters of the far north, including these Canadian Inuit, want to have control of their own land.

6 Peoples of the forest

The effect of the destruction of the world's rain forests on the peoples who live in the forest is rarely mentioned. Yet it is their home, and they are greater experts than any scientist on its creatures and plants.

There are forest peoples in South America, Africa, India, New Guinea, the Philippines and all over southeast Asia. Some of them are hunter-gatherers, like the "pygmy" peoples of central Africa. Most, however, combine hunting and fishing with growing crops by "swidden," or "slash-and-burn," farming. A patch of forest is cleared and planted; after one or two seasons' cultivation, the land is left to become forest once again, and the farmers clear a new area. Swidden is the best way to use the tropical forest soils, provided the land is left long enough for the forest to grow back properly. If, because land is running short, the farmers go back too soon to the same patch, it will rapidly lose its fertility. As one elder from the Philippines put it:

The settlers plant on one piece of land until the earth there becomes weak. We move to different areas before the earth gets too weak to grow our crops, and when we return to that spot the earth is even stronger.

The destruction of forests is causing concern worldwide, but what about the peoples of the forests? What will happen to them when their environment is destroyed?

Barricades in the forest

The Penan of the Sarawak forest led the protest against its destruction by loggers.

Sarawak is part of the island of Borneo, in southeast Asia. It is the largest state in the Federation of Malaysia. Much of Sarawak was once covered with trees and contained perhaps the richest diversity of plant and animal life in all the world's tropical forests, and today the interior is still heavily forested.

Nearly half of Sarawak's population consists of the tribal peoples known as the Dayak – the Penan, Kelabit, Kayan, Kenyah, Berewan and Iban. The Penan are the last nomadic hunter-gatherers of the region. The remainder are more settled people, living along the many rivers and cultivating rice and other crops on the hillsides. Most of them practice traditional swidden agriculture. Their dwellings are the famous Dayak long houses, where whole communities live under one roof, with each family occupying a room along a common veranda. Both nomads and settled farmers depend on the forest as the basis for their life. Their most cherished traditions and spiritual beliefs are centered on their relationship to the land. But the laws of Sarawak give the forest peoples no control over the land they believe is theirs.

Today, the greatest threat to Sarawak's native peoples is logging, the cutting down of the forest for its valuable lumber. Deforestation in Malaysia is going on faster than anywhere else in the world and, within Malaysia, Sarawak is the state most severely affected. Logging is the single largest source of revenue for the Sarawak state government, and government ministers, their relations, and foreign contractors are growing rich on the profits. At least 30 percent of Sarawak has already been logged, and 60 percent is leased out by the government to the logging companies. Experts believe that

The Dayak peoples make up almost half the population of Sarawak.

if this goes on, logging in Sarawak will be finished in ten years – there will not be any true forest left. When the trees are cut down, the forest animals disappear and, without the tree roots to hold it, the earth is washed down into the rivers, causing them to silt up and the fish to die.

But the native peoples of Sarawak are resisting what is being done to them and to their land. In early 1987 the last of the Penan nomads in the Baram region, a group who have been particularly hard hit by logging operations, issued an appeal to the government:

> Stop destroying the forest or we will be forced to protect it. The forest is our livelihood. We have lived here before any of you outsiders came. We fished in clean rivers and hunted in the jungle. We made our sago meat and ate the fruit of the trees. Our life was not easy, but we lived it in content. Now the logging companies turn rivers into muddy streams and the jungle into devastation. The fish cannot survive in dirty rivers and wild animals will not live in devastated forest.

Every minute, seven acres of forest are cut down in Malaysia.

> You took advantage of our trusting nature and cheated us into unfair deals. You take away our livelihood and threaten our very lives. You make our people discontent. We want our ancestral land, the land we live off, back. We can use it in a wiser way. When you come to us, come as guests, with respect.

When their appeals were ignored, the Penan acted. They set up barricades across the logging companies' roads, declaring: "Until we die we will block this road." Their lead was followed by several other Dayak groups, including the Kenyah, Kayan, Lunbawang and Kelabit peoples. The barricades lasted until October, when the authorities arrested 42 people. Meanwhile, however, the tribal campaign had caught the imagination of the world; articles appeared in newspapers everywhere, and people protested to the Malaysian government in support of the Dayak. In May 1988, the Penan and other tribal peoples put up their barricades once again. In July of the same year, the European Parliament passed unanimously a resolution urging countries to stop the import of tropical hardwoods from Malaysia until the logging was reduced and the native peoples' way of life respected.

Forest dwellers and gold-diggers

On the other side of the world, the Yanomami, whose lands straddle the border between Brazil and Venezuela, are also threatened. They live in one of the few remaining undisturbed large forests, an area of 60,000 square miles. Most of the forest tribes of South America have either been destroyed or reduced to a tiny number, like the Aché, and have had their way of life changed by contact with the whites. The Yanomami, however, have kept their culture and land intact. They have managed to do so because, until recently, the remoteness of their territory and their reputation for fierceness protected them from outside contact.

Numbering about 21,000, they live in some 360 settlements. Like the Dayak they support themselves by hunting with poisoned arrows, fishing and by slash-and-burn farming. Their characteristic form of settlement is the *yano*, a village that is one circular communal house with an open space up to 150 feet across in the center. Among the various *yanos* there may be

Once independent, the Brazilian Yanomami are now losing their land and their lives.

a constant threat of feud; but there are also alliances, exchanges of visits and feasting.

But underneath their territory gold and diamonds are buried. For years anthropologists, missionaries and other concerned people have urged the Brazilian government to create by law a single large territory where the Yanomami and their forest could exist undisturbed. When in 1987 it looked as though this was actually going to be done, gold prospectors started pouring in, determined to beat the deadline. Now there is a real gold rush going on, and the big mining companies are waiting for their chance to join in. Moreover, the powerful Brazilian army wants to set up a military zone along the border with Venezuela. In the first part of 1988, 75 Yanomami had already died from epidemics of flu, malaria and measles, caught from the miners, and poisoning from the mercury used in the gold extraction process.

7 Looking forward

In the previous chapters we have seen that cultures all over the world are threatened for much the same reasons. These reasons are partly political: governments wish to safeguard their own power, and are afraid that minority groups may try to split away from them or support a rebel movement or foreign power. Anyone who is "different" is suspected of being a traitor. Governments are also determined to protect their frontiers with military installations, or to exercise their bombers or test nuclear weapons in remote places, taking little account of the local people.

Other reasons are economic, and have to do with the growing pressure on land and those things on or under the land that people want or need. In particular, the parts of the world where tribal or indigenous peoples live, formerly thought of as "wilderness" by others, contain some of the materials that are most in demand today. Miners, oil workers, loggers, cattle ranchers, owners of large plantations and peasants wanting new land for their small plots all move in. Soon there are so many settlers that they turn the original people of the land into a minority. Hydroelectric projects with huge dams flood whole valleys, turning the inhabitants off their lands: on the Narmada River in India, for instance, a planned series of dams will flood the lands of 60,000 tribal people.

A people's culture may be destroyed by those who are hostile to them or simply do not care. But sadly the same thing can be done by people whose intentions are good. Europeans have always thought that their own culture was the only real one; hence they were determined to "assimilate" the Native Americans or the Australian Aborigines. Today the Muslim Indonesian government, in the name of its culture, is intent on doing the same thing to the people of West Papua.

There are some Christian missionaries who believe that, to convert people to Christ, they must turn them into exact copies of Western people, though other missionaries encourage them to keep their own culture and work to support their rights. In the past, missionaries have converted "heathen" people by force, destroying their shrines and sacred objects; and recently the Chinese were doing the same thing in Tibet to turn Buddhists into Communists. Both groups, of course, believed that they were fighting for goodness and saving the people from evil.

Armed conflict not only kills people, it also destroys cultures.

Tourists, also, are well-meaning people who may do damage without intending to. Far from wanting to destroy foreign cultures, they want to see and enjoy them – but with the danger of turning them into a permanent sideshow. And the scenes they gaze at and photograph, whether monasteries in Tibet or Bushmen camps, may not be all that they seem.

How can a culture be preserved?

Threatened cultures by definition belong to people who are comparatively poor and powerless, and some of them are among the poorest and most oppressed in the world. Control of culture lies in the hands of those who are wealthy and powerful. This means, among other things, that to preserve their own culture,

People who intend to help save a culture often unintentionally contribute to its destruction.

people under threat must have some kind of political independence – a right to run their own lives – which need not necessarily mean being a completely separate state. Many of the peoples we have looked at are numerically much too small to be separate states in the world of today. (The world of tomorrow may be different – who knows?) So an important question is, what sort of independence can such peoples have inside a larger state?

We said at the beginning of this book that keeping your culture means keeping the right to choose how and whether to change; so without political rights, "culture" becomes simply a kind of hobby, preserving folk dances and so

Minorities need to organize to protect their future, as have these Canadian Indians.

on. For this reason, one of the most important things is for a people to be able to set up their own organizations to speak for them, as more and more minorities are doing, including indigenous or tribal groups.

Generally, the first and most basic requirement in order that people can safeguard their culture and remain a people is rights over their land. This includes nomadic people who need hunting or grazing rights, and travelers like Gypsies who need the right to camping places. (For one can have rights over land and still share it with others.)

What is progress?

"But," some people will say, "surely you can't stand in the way of progress? Isn't it inevitable that these peoples and their cultures must disappear?"

It depends on what you mean by progress. In many ways the modern world seems to have taken a wrong turning – with pollution and destruction of nature, great poverty alongside great wealth, huge cities full of crime, squalor and lonely people. We have many wonderful machines, but they do not necessarily bring us

happiness. Perhaps we can learn something from the peoples that we used to dismiss as primitive and backward.

And is the disappearance of their cultures so inevitable? Is progress like some huge machine that rolls along into the future regardless of human beings, or can we perhaps steer it? Is it not up to us, the human race, to decide what kind of future we want? And do we really want a future in which everyone dresses, behaves and thinks just the same?

"Our old people," says George Erasmus of the Dene Indians, "when they talk about how the Dene ways should be kept by young people, when they talk about our land claims, they are not looking back, they are looking forward. They are looking as far ahead into the future as they possibly can. So are we all."

What to do

If you are concerned for the peoples of the world whose cultures and rights are threatened, the first thing you can do is to learn more about them and understand more about the issues, for a book like this can only scratch the surface of the problems. You can get in touch with the organizations that represent these peoples; and there are other organizations whose business it is to support peoples whose rights are threatened. (You will find a list of addresses at the back of this book.)

However, the problem is not just something on the other side of the world; it is on our doorstep, among our neighbors. If we can learn to be open-minded, and treat what is strange as interesting and beautiful rather than comic or nasty, and to love and value our own culture while respecting those of others, then we have made a start.

> To break the lamp of any people is to deprive it of its rightful place in the world's festival.
>
> *Rabindranath Tagore*
> *poet from India*

Glossary

Aborigines   The original inhabitants of a country, especially of Australia.

Assimilate   To encourage or force a person or group to become exactly like one's own group and blend in with it.

Colonization   The act by which one country takes power over another, generally in order to settle its own people there.

Deforestation   Destruction of forests.

Economic   To do with the making and management of wealth and money.

Elder   An older person respected for his or her wisdom, who acts as a leader.

Ethnocide   The destruction of the culture of a people.

Genocide   The killing of a whole group or race of people.

Guerrillas   Unofficial armed forces, generally fighting to remove a government.

Heathen   A person who does not believe in the God worshiped by Jews, Christians and Muslims.

Indigenous   Born in, or native to, a country.

Left-wing   In favor of changing society in the direction of socialism or Communism.

Minority   A part of a population that is different in race, culture or religion, and smaller or less powerful than the rest.

Mystic   One who experiences or tries to get in touch with a reality beyond the everyday world.

Nation-state   A country that is ruled by one central government and, in theory, consists of one people only. In fact nearly all nation-states contain more than one people.

Primitive   Once meant "to do with early times"; now generally used to mean undeveloped or crude.

Reservations (Reserves)   Areas of country set aside for groups of native people when the rest has been taken over by others. Sometimes, though not always, a reservation is part of the original land of the group concerned.

Right-wing   Opposed to change in society; in particular, opposed to socialism.

Sago   A starchy food made from the stem of the sago palm tree.

Sovereignty   The right or power to govern.

Traditional   According to custom or handed down from the past.

Treaties   Agreements between nations or groups.

Picture acknowledgments

Bryan and Cherry Alexander 28; Associated Press 16, 21; John Borthwick 7, 19, 38; David Bowden Photographic Library 18; C.J. Gibb/Chapel Studios Picture Library 20; Bruce Coleman Ltd 15, 23, 27 (top and bottom), 37, 39, 40; Mary Evans Picture Library 10, 11; Robert Harding Associates 31, 41; Hutchison Library frontispiece, 6, 13, 14, 24, 25, 36, 43, 44; Orde Eliason/Link cover, 32, 33, 34; Network Photographers 8; Christine Osborne 17, 29; Oxfam 42; Rex Features 12, 26, 30. Survival International 35. Artwork on page 8–9 provided by Swanston Graphics.

Books to read

Series

The Original Peoples series published by Rourke Publications includes books on the Inuit, Maoris, Aborigines, Bedouin, Plains Indians of North America, South Pacific Islanders, Indians of the Andes, Indians of the Amazon, Bushmen of the Kalahari and Pygmies of Central Africa.

The Cultural Geography series published by Watts includes information on some of the threatened cultures introduced in this book. Titles are *Living in Deserts, Living in Polar Regions, Living in the Tropics,* and *Living on Islands.*

Other Books

Children of the Maya: A Guatemalan Indian Odyssey, Brent Ashabranner (Dodd, Mead, 1986).

Growing Up Masai, Tom Schachtman (Macmillan, 1981).

Gypsies, Thomas Acton (Silver, 1985).

Morning Star, Black Sun: The Northern Cheyenne Indians and American's Energy Crisis, Brent Ashabranner (Dodd, Mead, 1982).

To Live in Two Worlds: American Indian Youth Today, Brent Ashabranner (Dodd, Mead, 1984).

Reports

"Forest Indians of South America," "Nothing to Celebrate," "Australian Aborigines Today," and "Tribal Peoples in Indonesia," all from Survival International.

Periodicals

Akwesasne Notes available from Mohawk Nation, Rooseveltown, New York, 13683. Deals mainly with Native Americans but covers indigenous peoples worldwide.

Cultural Survival Quarterly (address below). Informative articles on threatened peoples.

Further information

If you wish to find out more about some of the subjects covered in this book, you might find the following addresses useful:

Cultural Survival
11 Divinity Avenue
Cambridge MA 02138

Supports projects to help indigenous peoples and publishes reports and a quarterly journal.

International Campaign for Tibet
1151 K Street NW, Suite 739
Washington DC 20005

Survival International USA
2121 Decatur Place NW
Washington DC 20008

Campaigns for the rights of threatened indigenous peoples and publishes quarterly newsletters as well as a series of special reports.

World Council of Indigenous People
555 King Edward Avenue
Ottawa
Ontario
Canada

Index

The numbers in **bold** refer to the pictures.